wildflowers

Bailey Rae

Cover designed by Bailey Rae
Cover images via Unsplash

Illustrations by Bailey Rae

Second paperback edition February 2022

ISBN 978-0-6452021-3-7 (paperback)

Published by Bailey Rae
www.baileyraebooks.com

br

Bailey Rae | Author

to everyone who loves me,
demons and all.

and for james,
who believed in me more than anyone.

i have been hurt
many times
in many kinds
by many people

and i have felt loss
so sudden
it tore a hole
in my soul
that will not mend

but

i have also felt love
many times

in many kinds

by many people

and for them
i have tried to fill
the empty spaces
in my heart
with words

and now

i have put them all
down on paper
to share with you
in hopes
that maybe
they will help you
start to heal too

flowers

i don't remember
how it feels
to have the sun
on my skin
to feel it's warmth
or to have hope that
there are brighter days
still to come

i feel like
these storm clouds
above my head
have always been there
casting me
in eternal shadow

his love
was barbed wire
coiled around my heart
so tight
for so long
that i didn't know
love
should feel
like anything else

i ripped my heart to shreds
trying to fix yours
but for every tear i'd mend
you would make
two more

(one for you. one for me.)

you can't fix what's in tatters
i wish i'd realised that before
because now my heart
looks just like
yours

i am drowning

and i have been
holding my breath
fighting the current
trying to get my head
back above water

but i never could swim
and i've been under for so long
that i can't help but think
maybe it would be easier
if i just opened my mouth
and let the water
fill my lungs

some days
i stay silent
because i am
afraid
that if i try
to speak
all i will do
is scream

he was a wildfire
burned bright
and fast
and free

and i was
so mesmerised
by his light
that i didn't think
to run
when his flames
kissed my skin
and tried to burn me too

i would be anything you wanted
as long as it meant
i got to be
your
something

even if
that meant
i
became
nothing

he loved
my body
so much
that all
i could do
was hate it

i sit on the moon
fishing for stars
casting a line
and waiting
waiting
w a i t i n g
to catch a dream

i looked at you
like you put the stars
in the sky
and i was
so naive
that i didn't realise
each star you hung
so meticulously
you plucked
from my eyes

you made me promises
warm and golden
and i basked
in the sunlight
of your lies

your love came with conditions
like:
i had to love you
unconditionally
and i didn't see a problem with that

your ivy has conquered
my field of daisies

.

would it be okay
if i never quite make it
to *okay*?

- *would you still love me?*

sometimes i think
i see a light
up ahead
and then i hear
the devil laugh
and i realise
it was all
just
a mirage

i bury myself
in busy days
no time to stop
and feel

because

in the quiet moments

when i'm alone

that's when the demon
that hides in
the deepest corners of my soul
crawls out

and he comes for me

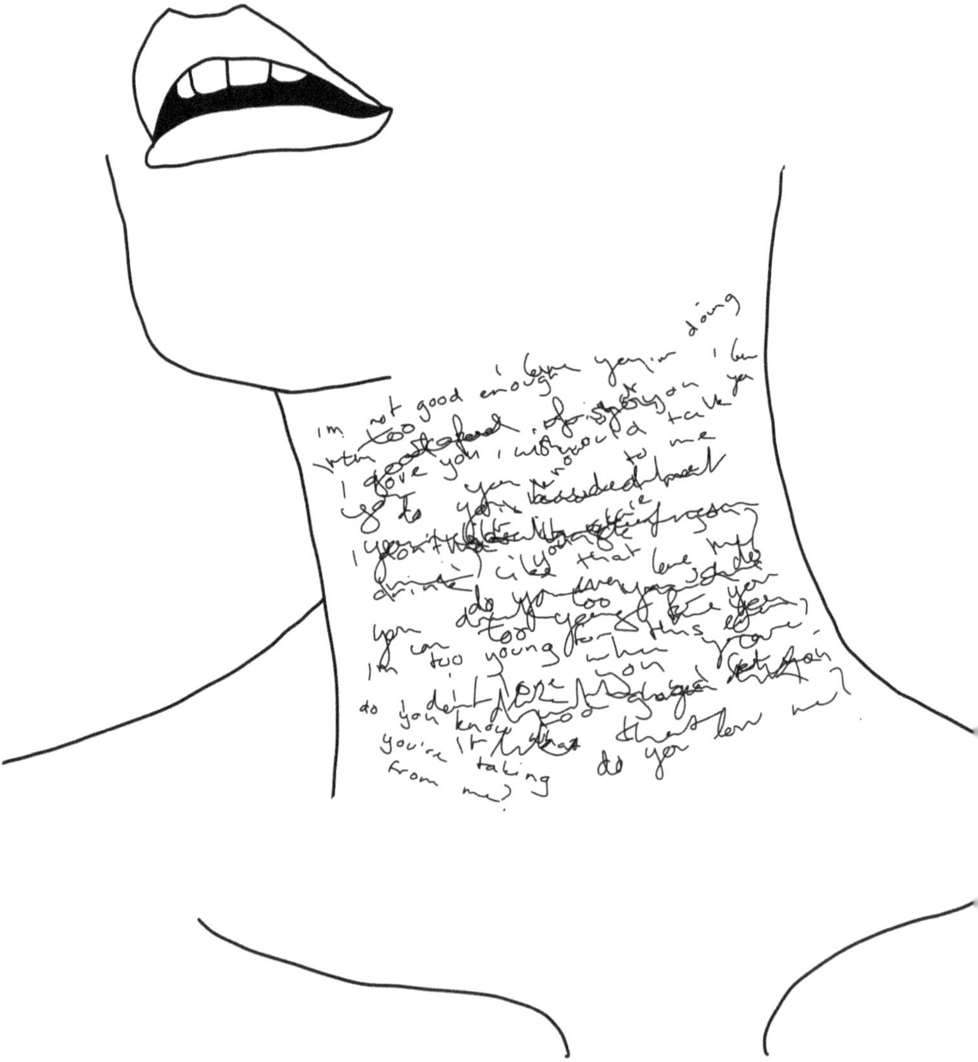
i'm not good enough
i love you
i'm too young
you're taking from me?

all the things
i am too scared to say
are stuck in my throat
and i am
suffocating on them

- *i would rather choke than tell you the truth*

he was once
the brightest star
but the light inside of him
died

he became a black hole
and the force of him
was so strong
that it took all of her love
and all of her light
and she never had
any hope
of escape

i wanted to bask
in the light of your sun
i wanted to throw my head back
let your heat warm my skin
and start to thaw
this frozen heart

but my skin never thickened
so when i turned to you
and stripped myself bare
all you did
was burn

if i gave you all of me
it wouldn't be enough

- but it's all i have

i painted myself
in shades of blue
because you said
it looks good on you

you saw me in the wild
and wanted me for yourself
so you took me home
put me in a vase
in the middle of a shelf
and showed me off
to all of your friends
but a flower only lasts
so long
once it's pulled from the ground
and you threw me away
when i started to wilt

- leave me as i am and i will bloom for a lifetime

someday
i'll want back
all the pieces of me
i ever gave
to you

but for now
you can keep them
because i don't know
how to be
whole

i envy the birds who
make nests in my branches
and find shelter in my leaves
who can fly away to
wherever they'd like
whenever they'd like
while i stay here
forever growing
but rooted
to the ground

you broke me down
so many times
that my sharp edges
softened

now i'm a ghost
of who i once was
and who i could've been
is unrecognisable

yet still
you take me apart

only now
not even you
know how
to put me back together

i wish i didn't let myself
get so lost in you
because now you're gone
and i don't know how to find
me

i hold
entire constellations
within my soul

but all he saw
were the stars
in my eyes

they say a girl's first love
will be just like her father

so i suppose that is why
i fell for a man
who bought happiness off the street
and tried to inject it
directly into his veins

a man who
had no love of his own
so he spent every night searching for it
at the bottom of a bottle

i suppose that is why
i fell for a man
who only knew how to love me
by hurting me first

i have mastered the art of smiling
when all i want to do is scream

i would sell my soul
just to feel
something
other than lonely

but the devil didn't want me either

we are stars under the same sky
and yet galaxies apart

isn't it strange
to think there was a time
i didn't know you at all

and isn't it stranger
to think there was a time
when all i knew was you

i gave you all my love
because you needed it more than i did
and i thought that
when the time came
you would give a little back

i was just a rosebud
hadn't finished growing
didn't have any thorns
to ward you off
when you wrapped your hands around me
and pulled me from the earth

by the time you put me back
the damage had been done
and i'm fully grown now
(thorns and all)
but my petals have been tarnished
crushed by your closed fists

and now
i will never be
quite as beautiful
as those who grew before me
or those who will grow after

i only miss you at night
when the sky goes dark
and the moon lights up
and i can no longer ignore
this hollow feeling
that's haunted my soul
ever since you left
to join the stars

your future always looked so bright
and the light in mine went out with you

losing you
was like losing a limb

- i still feel the phantom pain

i wasted so much time
hating the person
i saw in the mirror
now you're gone
and i have no proof
that we ever existed
in the same time
and space

sometimes i wonder
in some
parallel universe
is it me
who was forced
into an endless sleep
and you
who is trapped
in an endless mourning?

i'm afraid i'll forget
the way you laughed
because when
that sound
no longer
plays
on a loop
in my head
you
will
really
be
g o n e

you had a head start
but i have travelled
around the sun
more times
than you
ever
will

we were:

two halves
one whole

two peas
one pod

the sun
and the moon

a yin
and a yang

i haven't been complete
since you've been gone

- *i miss you every day*

everything happens for a reason
that's what they say
so tell me
what was the purpose of
tearing you from this earth
and
ripping you out of my life
just to put you
in the ground?

my head is at war with my heart
and no matter who wins

i lose

the things i do
to keep the demon at bay
have become a part
of the demon itself

i learned too much too young

i learned that men will stare
no matter where you go
or what you wear
and that they don't care
how young you are

i learned to be afraid
of a raised voice
and the raised fist
of the man
who should've been
my protector

i learned how it felt to starve
and to sacrifice
and to be the protector
when i could barely protect myself

i learned how it felt to fear
walking down the street
and my father's rage
and my mother's guilt

i learned to be alone
but not in any of the ways
it really matters

but the hardest thing
i had to learn
was that
none of the other children
had to learn
any of this

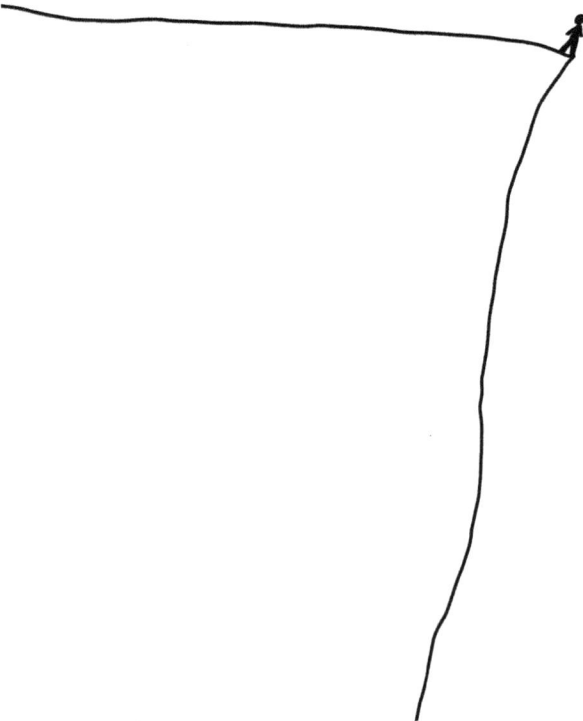

the problem
is that
i can no longer
tell the difference
between how it feels
to fly
and how it feels
to fall

- but i take the jump anyway

i sit in darkness
because i know it
i've made friends
with the shadows on the walls

i sit in darkness
because there
we are all the same
fumbling blindly with our arms out

i sit in darkness
because i'd rather be
blissfully unaware of
the evil things that hide with me

i sit in darkness
because i don't know
what awaits me
if i step into the light

where do you keep your sadness?

do you keep it in your heart
and pin it proudly to your sleeve?

do you keep it in your head
and soldier on, unbothered?

or are you like me?

do you keep it in your soul?

so heavy
it weighs you down
down
d o w n

until you can no longer move?

when i look into the mirror
all i see is my past
and the smile that i wear
can't hide the inner scars
but no one else can see them
so i put back on the mask
when all i really want to do
is put my fist through the glass

they always said
i was the brightest star
in the cluster
but no one warned me
i would be the first
to burn out

i cross the road
without looking
because the risk
is the only thing
that reminds me
how much i want
to live

face your demons
that's what they said
so i packed up my hope
and trudged through
my desolate soul
to knock on his door

when my demon answered
his eyes so dark
twinkled with mischief
and with irises like the night sky
looking at him
felt like stargazing

then he smiled at me
with so much ardour
that i smiled right back
because i didn't think
that something truly evil
could look like an angel

but he made me feel warm
and he made me feel welcome

so when he opened the door
to his house of mirrors
i stepped inside
and made myself at home

i am tired
of feeling shame
and taking blame
and childish games
and everything staying the same

i am tired
of storms raging
and wars waging
and nothing ever changing
and finding everything disengaging

i am tired
of my bones aching
and my confidence shaking
and my spirit breaking
and every day, of waking

i am tired

- just let me sleep

i turned my pain into prose
now they call my words beautiful
but still they close their eyes
at the sight of my scars

my mind is a garden i forget to weed. i want to write some aesthetic rhyme but i can't find the right words amongst the foliage. my mind is a garden, with pansies for my thoughts because i am *free* and roses for my words because they're beautiful but they're *sharp* and white lilacs in a special pot tucked in the corner for my younger self, because i didn't get enough time with her. my mind is a garden. it's bright and it's colourful and it's so, *so* beautiful when it blooms. my mind is a garden, but i don't tend to it like i should. i don't water it enough, i don't whisper kind words to my flowers like people tell me to. i have ivy growing up the walls of my greenhouse and i like that it keeps people out, but it traps me in. daffodils litter my flowerbeds like little spots of sun. they shine so bright amongst the dark leaves, i forget they're poison. their sap soaks through to my roots, seeps into the foundations of my mind and kills all the beautiful things that i spent so long growing. and before i even think to stop it, all my plants are dead. so i sew new seeds and i start all over again. my mind is a garden i forget to weed.

wild

to the person i see in the mirror:
i'd love to get to know you.

you left me
in the dirt
thinking it would
bury me
but mother nature
nurtured me
she took me in
kissed my wounds
with midnight moss
and morning dew
i became one
with the earth
and from the ground
i *bloomed*

you can hurt me if you'd like
i have learned to grow flowers
out of the wounds you leave

you kept me silent for so long
i forgot i had a voice
so i learned to speak
without saying anything at all

here you are crying
begging me for sympathy
when every awful thing
you have ever said
or done to me
is burned into
the back of my eyelids
and
it's all i see
when i close my eyes

and if i was the kind of person
i sometimes wish i could be
(the kind of person *you* are)
i would use it all
to make you feel
lonely
and cold

i would rub salt
in all of your wounds
and i would make you
feel worse
and worse
until somehow
on one cosmic plane
or another
we were even

but i won't

you have broken me down
and built me back up
now i am a lego house
only you know how to build

and i will not
do the same to you

your heart
is no place
for hatred

for James

1997 – 2016

i don't mind the hurting
if it means i can remember
how it felt to love you
and be loved by you

he was an earthquake
shook my world to it's core
destroyed my foundations
but from the rubble
i will rise

and i will rebuild

i don't need you to ask me
if i'm okay
i just need you
to remind me
that one day
i will be

you sacrificed your youth
for his promise of family
you scooped up your future
and gave it to me

you didn't know then
that you would grow to regret
the possibilities you lost
the dreams you can't forget

you gave me life
and it came with a sentence
now you drink too much wine
and you beg for repentance

but no one was ready
not even you
so for giving me breath
mother, i forgive you

i know i cannot
turn back time
but it has been
one-thousand
six-hundred
and twenty-one days
since you last laid your
ungrateful hands
on me

now
i just need to wait
another
nine-hundred
and thirty-four
until by body is one
that has never known you

you were always enough
but they were still growing
and their hands
could not hold you
just yet

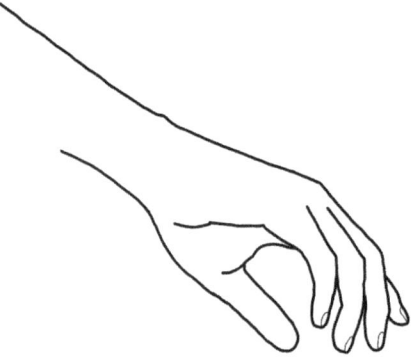

there is a fire in your soul
and a rage in your heart

simmering

simmering

s i m m e r i n g

until it boils over
and when it does
you call it love

well
i have been burned
by that thing you call *love*
a hundred times before
you can burn me again
for i am a phoenix

and from the ashes

i rise

you've picked up the shards
of your broken heart
and pieced them together
with golden lacquer
so many times before
you can do it once more
and with every new mess
it will hurt a little less

you don't say *i love you*. but you smile when i wear my hair that way. and you're frugal, but you buy me frivolous things worth more than anything my family has ever owned because you say i don't deserve anything less. and when i've had a long day at work, you buy me dinner and you put on my favourite show and you kiss me on the forehead and you say *my poor baby*. and every night you rub my back, because you know how my body aches. and every morning you hold me real tight (and you're so warm and i'm always running late, so i started setting my alarm a little earlier just to have more time with you). and every new years you kiss me at midnight, even when we're speeding along the highway on our way to the city because we spent too long lazing at home and you don't want me to miss the fireworks. you don't *say* you love me, but i've learned to speak your language.

the day i said goodbye to you
i said hello to me

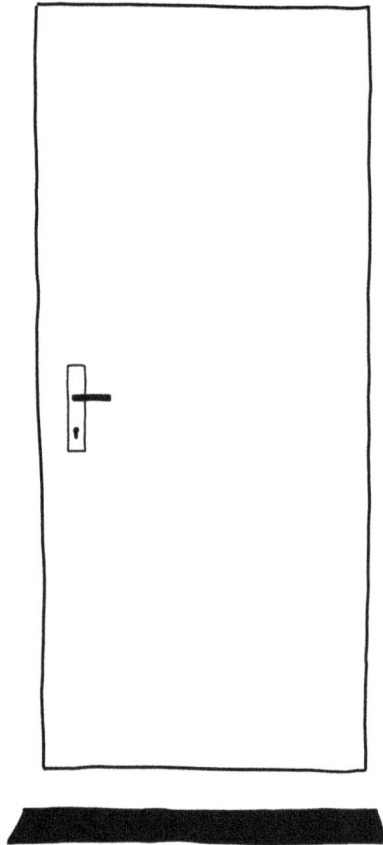

collect your sorrow
and gather your grief
build it a home
somewhere safe in your heart

make it light
make it warm
and visit there often
because pain gets lonely too

but don't stay too long
and don't forget
to lock the door behind you
when you leave

sometimes when i miss you
i howl at the silver moon
and it helps to think
you're out there somewhere
howling at it too

a picture is worth
a thousand words
and although i can't
talk to you anymore
i have entire albums
filled with your smile
saved in my mind
and i look at them
when it rains

we still exist
in my wildest dreams
in my most dangerous fantasies
in the way my cheeks flush
when i think of us

my love,
we were always
going to end
in tragedy
because
when i fell
you weren't there
to catch me
you were right
by my side
falling too

you and i existed in the *almost*

in the way i wanted you
even when you were taken

and in the way you wanted me
the whole time too

(in the way i fell in love with you
before i even knew your name)

but time was never on our side
and if i
could turn back the hands
on the clocks of our lives
i wouldn't

because you and i
existed

you know that time between asleep and awake?

just before the sun comes up
and the sky is still dark
and you're straddling worlds
with one foot in ours
and one still in a place
you can barely remember

that is when i think of you

i am a castle made of sand, and his love comes in waves. but i am not afraid. because i know that every time he tears me down, the people i love are waiting. and they are ready and willing to build me back up, stronger and even more breathtaking than i was before.

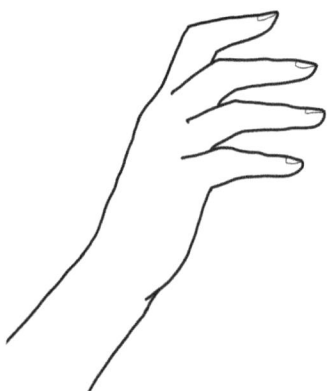

i know the stars
are out of my reach
but you make me believe
i can touch the sky

sometimes i think
what if i really am nobody?
and then you look at me
and suddenly
i am everything

we have fallen
for the ideas
and the ideals
of each other
rather than
the realities
and soon
this fire will
burn out
but when
we do
darling
we will take
entire cities
down
with us

i fell in love with you
the moment i learned
what love was

up in the clouds
is where my dreams lie

i spend my days in a haze
gazing up at the sky

and they say *there is no way!*
but they do not know my might

i am more than they think
i am learning to fly

so just you wait, say goodbye
before long i'll be gone

i'll be up in the clouds
i'll be where i belong

i never learned how to swim
but i would dive into you
and drown in your oceans
if only you would ask

i love you the way the moon loves the tide

- *from a distance*

with a mouth
full of stardust
you say i am
your universe
so come
paint my cosmos
with the stars
on your tongue

i didn't know who i was
until he took the time
to remove every mask

one

by

one

and his hands were so gentle
and his eyes were so warm
that i didn't even notice
when i looked in the mirror
all that was left

was *me*

will you share this crown with me?

my head
is starting
to get
heavy

your eyes say more than my words ever could.

i fell in love with a shooting star

- *beautiful, but fleeting*

you are the sun
don't waste your warmth
on people searching for shade

i was lost in the woods
feet raw from running
when you found me
and you took me in
and you kissed my wounds
and you left the door unlocked
so that i could leave
if i wanted
but you cared for me so well
and you made me feel so safe
that i never
wanted

i needed to fall apart
it is how i learned
to piece myself
back together

i took a chisel
to the chip on my shoulder
and carved myself
into something new

you were forged
in fire and brimstone
and i know you think
that makes you weak

but darling

you survived

and that
is what makes you

s t r o n g

i have been
torn apart

but

if i give
what's left
of *me*
to *you*

maybe

you could
make something
beautiful

.

i consider myself
far luckier
than dear atlas
for my world is much smaller
and i am strong enough
to carry
the weight
of *you*

The callouses on his palms, rough
Our hands intertwined
Under covers, late at night.
Clumsy kisses and
His breath warm on my skin.

Stormy nights in july
Crisp august air and
Early morning petrichor.
Nostalgia by the fireplace,
Timber smoke smells like home.

Sunday sun seeping through the blinds,
Iridescent butterflies and
Golden sunsets on the horizon.
Heavenly skies put stars in our eyes, they're
Twinkling as we count constellations.

Soft voices on midnight drives,
Our song on the radio and
Unknown words, we sing them still.
Never ending lullabies, his
Dulcet tones sing me to sleep.

The sweat on his skin
And his lips,
Saccharine sweet.
Tea at midnight while i write,
Every morning fresh brewed coffee.

i am alive.

i am a sunflower
and you must be too
because when the sun goes down
i turn to you

i know your head
gets loud sometimes
but i'll keep screaming
i love you
in hopes that
it will drown out
some of the noise

i will love you

even when you can't love me
especially when you can't love yourself

i will love you
i will love you
i will love you

- just like you did for me

people come and go
but you are stuck
with *you*
forever
the least you can do
is be kind to yourself

i am learning to accept myself
as i am
now
between the person i was
and the person i am trying to be

you will never know
how enchanting
your voice is
until you stop trying
to sing along
with everyone else

we were all born
with hearts for feeling
and heads for thinking
and some of us
were lucky enough
to be born with
the good sense
to use them both

please be patient
i am still learning
to love myself

one look at you
and it's like coming up for air
after i've been drowning
for so long

words can hurt
and words can heal.

i have been hurt
so i choose to heal.

in the middle of the night
when i'm alone in our bed
and the darkness
is closing in
threatening
to swallow me whole
he comes
and he wraps his arms around me
and the darkness retreats
and everything is calm
and i can't imagine
love
could feel
like anything else

do not mistake your cocoon
for a coffin
your journey has just started
and soon enough
you will emerge from the darkness
fully grown
a magnificent butterfly
and your wings will cast shadows
on all of those
who ever doubted your beauty

thank you

About the Author

Bailey Rae is a storyteller, poet, dreamer born in Western Australia. She currently resides in the outer suburbs of Melbourne, Australia with her partner and the love of her life — a pug named Hunny. *wildflowers* is not only her first collection of poetry, but her first published work. It will not be the last.

www.ingramcontent.com/pod-product-compliance
Lightning Source LLC
Chambersburg PA
CBHW030823090426
42737CB00009B/846